A souvenir guide

Stowe
Buckinghamshire

GW00570814

'A Work to wonder at' 2
4   Power gardening
6   Stowe stories
8   Making you welcome
10 On the grandest scale

Exploring Stowe 12
12 The Corinthian Arch
12 The New Inn
13 The Bell Gate
13 The South Front of the House
13 The Path through Life

The Path of Vice 14
14 The Lake Pavilions
14 The Hermitage
15 The Temple of Venus
16 The Queen Caroline Monument
16 The Sleeping Parlour
17 The Rotondo
17 The Temple of Bacchus
18 St Augustine's Cave
19 The Vanbrugh Pyramid
19 Dido's Cave
19 The George II Monument

The Path of Virtue 20
20 The Elysian Fields
21 The Doric Arch
21 The Temple of Modern Virtue
21 The Temple of Ancient Virtue
22 The Grenville Column
22 The Grotto
23 Captain Cook's Monument
23 The Temple of British Worthies
24 The Queen's Temple
25 The Cobham Monument
25 The Chinese House

The Path of Liberty 26
26 The Temple of Concord
        and Victory
26 The Grecian Valley
27 The Wolfe Obelisk
27 The Bourbon Tower
28 The Saxon Deities
28 Hawkwell Field
29 The Gothic Temple
30 The Palladian Bridge
31 The Temple of Friendship
31 Stowe Castle

Looking to the Future 32

❋ National Trust

'A Work to wonder at'

Spontaneous beauties all around advance,
Start ev'n from Difficulty, strike from Chance;
Nature shall join you, Time shall make it grow
A Work to wonder at – perhaps a Stow.'

Alexander Pope, *Epistle to Burlington*, 1731

In its late 18th-century heyday, Stowe was the most magnificent landscape garden in Britain. Indeed, it rivalled the grandest royal gardens of continental Europe. The Temple family, who owned Stowe, spent a fortune creating and extending the garden to further their political ambitions. They employed the most talented architects and garden designers of the age, together with a small army of staff, in order to ensure that they remained in the forefront of gardening fashion.

Follow in the footsteps
Always keen to show off, the Temples opened the garden to visitors from the 1730s. Many came, toured the garden and recorded their impressions, some of which are quoted in this guide. They spread Stowe's reputation throughout Britain and the world, so that you can now find versions of its most famous features from Russia to the United States.

Where are the flowers?
Today, gardening is largely about cultivating flowers of every hue. Eighteenth-century landscape gardens such as Stowe dealt in shades of green. Rolling expanses of grass were framed by artfully placed belts of trees and shrubs and reflected in tranquil stretches of water. Contrasting with these were garden buildings in classical and Gothic styles, which were ornamented with sculptures and inscriptions that delivered political and social messages to the discerning viewer. This guide will help you to unravel some of the complex stories of Stowe.

Above The south front of the house

Right The Temple of Ancient Virtue in 1848

Opposite The Gothic Temple

Decline and fall

Stowe reached its social peak in 1822, when Richard Grenville was created 1st Duke of Buckingham. In 1845 the family laid on an extravagant welcome for Queen Victoria, when she toured the garden. But only three years later, the 2nd Duke was declared bankrupt, and many of the contents of the house and garden were sold.

Step back in time

Stowe was rescued in 1923, when it was transformed into a school, and in 1990 the National Trust took over responsibility for the gardens. In 1997 the Stowe House Preservation Trust was created. Much has changed since Stowe's great 18th-century days, but much remains or has returned. Stowe is one of the very few places in Britain where you can still immerse yourself completely in Georgian magnificence on the grandest scale. Step back with us and be amazed.

Public virtue and private vice

At the heart of Stowe lies the complex personality of the soldier-politician Richard Temple, Lord Cobham. He took his politics very seriously, but was altogether more easy-going in matters of personal morality.

Timeline

1697	**Cobham** inherits Stowe
1715–19	French-style parterre south of the house
	Vanbrugh designs garden buildings
1717	New Inn built to accommodate visitors to Stowe
1720–25	Garden extended south to stream (which becomes the Octagon Lake) and west into Home Park
	Vanbrugh builds Rotondo
	Bridgeman's ha-ha encloses southern and western areas of the garden
1726	Vanbrugh dies
1726–32	Western Garden extended to full extent
	Eleven-acre Lake created
1733–9	Elysian Fields created: garden buildings by **William Kent**
1739–43	Hawkwell Field created: garden buildings by **James Gibbs**
1741	**'Capability' Brown** becomes head gardener
1743–9	Grecian Valley created
1749	Lord Cobham dies
1751	Brown leaves Stowe
1752	**Earl Temple** inherits Stowe on his mother's death
1760s	South Vista widened by felling Abele Walk
	Corinthian Arch built
1779	Earl Temple dies
1822	Richard Temple created 1st Duke of Buckingham
1848	2nd Duke almost bankrupt. Sale of contents of Stowe
1923	Stowe School founded
1990	National Trust given landscape garden

'The Stowe gardens 'are esteemed the *finest* of their *Kind* in England; & are indeed most *elegantly disposd*, & *beautifully diversifyed* with *Walks & Lawns, Canals & Grotto's, Waterfalls & various Buildings*, such as *Temples, Rotundas, Pyramids, Obelisks & Colonnades*.'

An anonymous visitor, 1735

Power gardening

The Stowe gardens were very largely the conception of two men: Viscount Cobham and his nephew and heir, Earl Temple.

Richard, Viscount Cobham (1675–1749)

Richard Temple's early years were devoted to a successful military career: he was promoted major-general in 1706 at the age of only 31. His knowledge of military fortification may have inspired the ha-has (sunken ramparts) which were such an important element of his garden. On the accession of George I in 1714 he was created Baron Cobham. His circle included not only leading architects and designers, but also some of the greatest literary figures of the age, including the poet Alexander Pope and the dramatist William Congreve. He was a welcoming host, but a stern landlord.

Bust of Viscount Cobham in a Roman toga

'My Lord [Cobham] is too great a Friend to Art to trust to Nature in her best Dressing, knowing how much the first would lose in the Comparison and her simple Beauties get the better of all his Vain Pomp.'

Jemima, Marchioness Grey, 1748

Richard, Earl Temple (1711–79)

Richard, Earl Temple, who inherited the estate in 1752, was proud and cantankerous in public. The king, George II, could not abide 'Squire Gawky', as he was called. But Temple's family letters reveal a much more sympathetic character, tender towards his relations, subject to fits of depression, and devoted to Stowe. He resented any time he had to spend in London, as it kept him away from his beloved gardens: 'I am extravagantly in love – with Stowe … never, never was any thing half so fine and charming', he admitted to his sister in 1761. He died following a carriage accident while being driven round the gardens.

Left Earl Temple; by William Hoare of Bath

Opposite left Sir John Vanbrugh; by Godfrey Kneller

Opposite right James Gibbs; by John Michael Williams

A political garden

Stowe reflected the Whig political views of its creators. The Whig party supported the Protestant religion and civil and political liberty. They backed the Glorious Revolution, which had brought the Protestant William III to power in 1688, and the succession of the Hanoverian dynasty in 1714. Sir Robert Walpole and his Whig party dominated politics in the early 18th century, but the Whigs splintered into many different and contending factions.

During the Excise Crisis of 1733 Lord Cobham fell out with Walpole and went into opposition, together with his numerous relations, who were known as 'Cobham's Cubs' and included two future prime ministers. Stowe is full of allusions to Cobham's political sympathies and to his friends and enemies.

From formality to freedom

At Stowe better than anywhere else you can trace the development of the English landscape garden during the 18th century from formality to freedom. It followed three broad phases:

- The royal gardener **Charles Bridgeman** laid out the bones of the garden from about 1714 with a series of straight, intersecting avenues and canals. He also devised the ha-ha, a combination of rampart and ditch that seamlessly connected the garden with the wider landscape beyond. Gardening fashion gradually turned against 'the stiffness of the old Bridgeman taste', as Earl Temple's cousin George Lyttelton put it.

- **William Kent** pioneered the next phase in the 1730s in the area known as the Elysian Fields (see p.20), where he devised a more informal and intimate effect. His careful combination of planting and garden temples created an essentially reflective mood.

- In the third phase, in the 1740s, **'Capability' Brown** worked on an even more ambitious scale, remodelling the landscape and planting to make the Grecian Valley (see p.26).

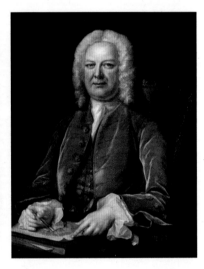

Sir John Vanbrugh

The greatest English architect of the Baroque era after Sir Christopher Wren, Vanbrugh is famous for designing Blenheim Palace and Castle Howard. For Stowe he devised a series of more modest, but still innovative and forward-looking garden buildings, including the Rotondo (p.17) and the Pyramid (the latter has now gone).

James Gibbs

Gibbs was a Catholic and a Tory, but was still happy working for great Protestant Whig landowners like Cobham. He focused mainly on the area known as Hawkwell Field, where he erected buildings and statues in the Gothic style that celebrated ancient English freedoms (see p.28).

Stowe stories

Moving temples and moving trees

Stowe was in a constant state of flux throughout the 18th century. Not even the buildings or the trees stood still. So, for instance, the little temple now known as the Fane of Pastoral Poetry began life as 'Gibbs's building' at the south-west corner of the garden and was surrounded by sculpture now incorporated into the Temple of British Worthies; it is now in the north-east corner of the garden. 'Capability' Brown invented a wagon that enabled him to dig up, transport and replant mature trees, so that he could transform the landscape with remarkable speed.

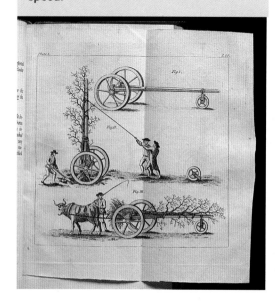

Right The South Portico in 1805; drawing by J.-C. Nattes

Below The Fane of Pastoral Poetry was moved from one end of the garden to the other

Under the portico

It is just after 12 o'clock on Thursday, 22 August 1805. The setting is the giant South Portico of the house – 'quite an orange grove', according to Betsey Fremantle, who was staying at Stowe for the visit of the Prince of Wales, which had drawn 10,000 people to the garden. Betsey's sister Harriet is talking to the Marquess of Buckingham's daughter, Lady Mary. They have much to discuss, as Mary is being courted by James Arundell, and her brother disapproves of the match, because Arundell is a Catholic. Betsey witnessed Mary and James's meeting under the portico the following day: 'The conversation which passed between them was most proper. Lady M. intreated him never to come back again, and explained matters so well, that he promised to go tomorrow without fail.' But love was not to be denied so easily: six years later, Mary and James were married.

A fatal accident

Stowe was a building site for much of the 18th century, and accidents were not uncommon. In September 1774 'the Whole Stone Cornish [cornice], upwards of Forty Foot across the End of the Centre of the House, over the *Drawing Room* we constantly sit in from having no other, Fell in', according to Catherine Stapleton. 'Divine Providence … has preserved us all except Poor Old Bachelor, the Stone Mason; He suffer'd but Momentary Pain or Fear.'

'In the keeping of [the garden], 12 men, 2 women and 8 boys are employ'd.'

John Evelyn, 1725

Making you welcome

Visitors have been encouraged to explore the constantly changing Stowe gardens for almost three centuries and have recorded their opinions of what they encountered.

Sophia, Lady Newdigate walks round Stowe in 1748

'They are copying the maison Quarré at Nismes a prodigious building [Temple of Concord and Victory] of which the foundation only is laid.

Lady Cobham is building a model of the Trajan Pillar to the honour of her Lord, on the Top of which is to stand a statue of him [Cobham Monument]. Every year great additions to the size of these gardens and to the crowd of buildings. The latter ones are in a much better taste than the former but if they were thinner sown would be much more pleasing to the eye. After walking between five and six miles we were heartily glad to get into the Coach where we refresh'd ourselves with a pot of Coffee.'

Below The Queen's Theatre from the Rotondo c.1733–4; by Jacques Rigaud

> 'I had taken up my abode at the New Inn … a pleasant hostelrie … wearing more the aspect of a snug farmhouse, than of a noisy comfortless inn.'
>
> Mary Sabilla Novello, 1825

The Prince of Wales visits Stowe in August 1805

'Dined at six and soon after nine, the Grotto being illuminated and the greatest concourse of people possible being assembled in the gardens, we all followed the Prince in Procession to the Grotto, …which had the appearance of enchantment, the Grotto and surrounding scene being illuminated most brilliantly, the Bridge and Obelisk on the water had a charming effect. Several Maskers were pitched on the banks, and groupes of Morice Dancers, the bands of the Pandeons, Savoyards and of the Regiments who were on the water played in succession, and enlivened the scene, the crowd was so great, there being at least 10,000 people present …. On the Prince's return to the Grotto the Fire works commenced and succeeded wonderfully well, the water rockets had a particular good effect and the whole went off with great éclat.'

Betsey Fremantle

Guidebooks to Stowe

This is only the latest in a long line of guidebooks to Stowe, which stretches back to the mid-18th century. The first guide to the gardens, which cost 6d, was published in 1744 by Benton Seeley, a Buckingham writing-master. He followed it in 1748 with *A Dialogue upon the Gardens*, which took the form of a discussion about the merits of the gardens between Callophylus (who loved nature improved by art) and Polython (who preferred nature in its raw state). Not surprisingly, Callophylus was more impressed by Stowe. Neither of these guides was illustrated, and so in 1750 Seeley produced a set of engravings of the temples. Seeley's various guides went through numerous editions, as he desperately tried to keep up with all the various changes to the gardens.

> 'Having now … paced better than Three Miles and a half, Ground enough, to make your Stomach by this Time, as much impatient to eat, as your Eye before was to see.'
>
> A visitor to Stowe in 1738

On the grandest scale

'Of all the gardens I have seen in England, this of Stowe appears to me to be the noblest and best planned.'

Henry Meister, 1799

Beyond the garden

The garden you see today may seem big enough, but it formed only a part of a much larger designed landscape. This covered over 5,000 acres in three counties, from Silverstone in the north to Buckingham in the south. It comprised farmland, deer-parks and woodland criss-crossed by great axial rides that are shown most dramatically on Sarah Bridgeman's 1739 survey map.

'The object of veneration to half the heathen world.'

Thomas Whateley, 1770

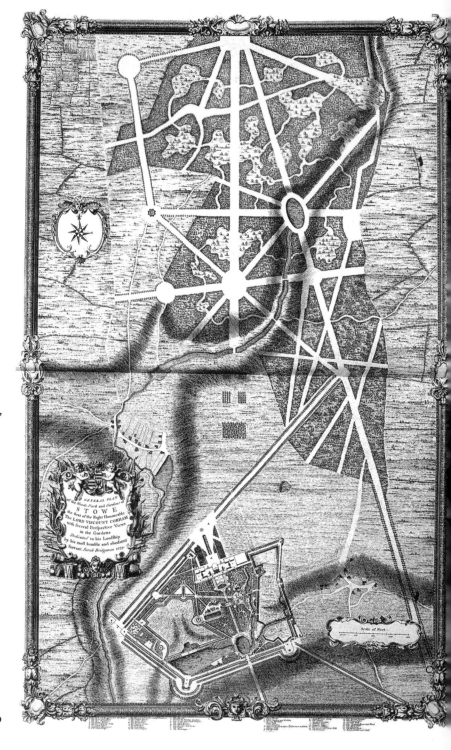

The influence of Stowe

The fame of the Stowe gardens was spread throughout Britain and beyond by impressed visitors and poetic eulogies; by published descriptions and engraved views in the Stowe guidebooks and elsewhere; and by the architects and designers who worked here. 'Capability' Brown made his reputation as head gardener at Stowe between 1741 and 1751, and went on to apply the lessons he had learnt here to countless great estates across Britain. In more recent times, the gardens have helped to shape generations of Stowe schoolboys in their formative years.

So many French enthusiasts visited Stowe that a French-language guidebook to the gardens was published in 1748. Back home, they created versions of Stowe at the Parc Monceau and the Désert de Retz. You can also find German translations of the Stowe temples at Wörlitz near Dessau. Perhaps Stowe's greatest fan was Catherine the Great of Russia, who created an English landscape garden on the Stowe model at Tsarskelo near St Petersburg and commissioned a Wedgwood dinner service decorated with numerous views of Stowe.

Above The Parc Monceau in France was strongly influenced by Stowe

Opposite Sarah Bridgeman's 1739 map of the vast designed landscape beyond the gardens

Exploring Stowe

'Oh! lead me to the wide extended walks,
The fair majestic paradise of Stowe!'

James Thomson, *Autumn*, 1744

The Corinthian Arch

The first of Stowe's famous collection of garden buildings that you encounter was also one of the largest and latest to be erected. It was designed in 1765 for Earl Temple by his cousin Thomas Pitt to frame a superb view of the south front of the house. It also had a practical function, providing accommodation for estate staff in the sides.

The New Inn

The New Inn was built by Lord Cobham in 1717 to accommodate visitors to the garden, which had already become a tourist attraction. Laid out around a central courtyard, it comprised a small brewery, a dairy and farm buildings as well as bedrooms for guests. Lord Perceval was not alone in complaining about the poor quality of the rooms, but it remained in use until the 1850s. The last innkeeper was Charles Bennet. Thereafter, it served as a farm until it was bought in 2005 by the National Trust, which has repaired the derelict fabric of the building and returned it to its original purpose as a place to welcome visitors.

Walk (or ride in the land train) from the New Inn down Bell Gate Drive to reach the gardens.

'Our Inn was a scurvy one and had not beds for all. Those of us who went to bed could not sleep for fleas and gnats.'

Viscount Perceval,
August 1724

Left The Corinthian Arch

Below The South Vista

The Bell Gate

This was the traditional entrance for visitors to the garden. You would ring the bell, and a boy would then take you round the garden in return for a small fee.

The South Front of the House

Stowe House is the grandest temple in the garden and, like the garden, was gradually extended and enriched over a century from 1683 until the South Front reached its present colossal scale, dominating the horizon. The core of the house was built by Sir Richard Temple in 1677–83, with pavilions to east and west linked to it by low screen walls. In the 1730s Lord Cobham rebuilt the pavilions and inserted columned galleries, which in the 1740s he replaced with magnificent suites of state rooms, in which he could impress and entertain his visitors. But at his death in 1749 he left the South Front an unsatisfactory muddle. The Duchess of Beaufort thought it 'a most extensive front being 1100 ft, but not either grand or pleasing'. Over the next 20 years Earl Temple employed a succession of leading architects – Borra, Blondel, Robert Adam – but rejected all their schemes in part or whole. Finally, he turned to his cousin Thomas Pitt, who managed to unify the immense façade with a single row of 48 Ionic columns and pilasters at first-floor (*piano nobile*) level, which thread behind three groupings of giant Corinthian columns and pilasters.

The Path through Life: The South Vista

At the Bell Gate entrance, you can enjoy a spectacular view of the South Vista. This is the physical, political and spiritual spine of the garden, around which everything else was planned. It links the centre of the South Front of the house up in front of you with the Corinthian Arch and the spire of Buckingham church behind you to the south. Whoever follows this route through the garden will be reminded at every step that they are treading the virtuous path through life. The statue of George I on horseback before the North Front of the house recalls the famous classical statue of the noblest Roman emperor, Marcus Aurelius. The Protestant and constitutional English monarch is also contrasted with the Catholic and absolutist French king, Louis XIV, creator of Stowe's greatest garden rival, Versailles. Prominent on the south front of the house are statues symbolising Peace and Plenty, Liberty and Religion. And the spire of Buckingham points towards the heaven that awaits those who have lived the good Protestant life. But before that, there are other choices to be made.

Left Statues symbolising Peace and Plenty decorate the South Front of the house

Below The equestrian statue of George I

Bottom *The Choice of Hercules*; by Nicolas Poussin

The Choice of Hercules

According to classical legend, the hero Hercules was faced with a moral choice. A seductive woman tries to persuade him to take the path of vice, which is superficially easier and more enjoyable. Meanwhile, another woman, dressed in sober white, points upwards to the more strenuous, but ultimately more satisfying, path to virtue.

On entering Bell Gate you are offered a similar choice. Turn left for the Garden of Vice. Turn right for the Garden of Virtue. Which path will you take?

The Path of Vice

Most of the buildings in the Western Garden are concerned with lust or unhappy or illicit love.

The Lake Pavilions:
Unrequited love

This pair of little temples, which frames the South Vista, may have been designed by Vanbrugh about 1719. They were moved apart in 1764, when Earl Temple widened the South Vista. The interiors were originally decorated by Francesco Sleter with murals on the theme of unrequited love taken from Guarini's play *Il Pastor Fido*, on which Handel based his popular opera, *The Faithful Shepherd*.

The Hermitage:
Sexual jealousy and melancholy

Spenser's *Faerie Queene* tells of the elderly Malbecco, who in despair and frustration took refuge in a hermitage like this after he had been deserted by his beautiful young wife, Hellinore (the episode depicted in the nearby Temple of Venus; see p.15). Cobham may have been poking fun at the 62-year-old Robert Walpole, who was to marry his young mistress Maria Skerrit in 1738. The Hermitage was designed by William Kent *c*.1731. With its roughly cut stone and dilapidated turret, it is an early example of a garden folly deliberately built as a ruin. The sombre surrounding planting adds to the melancholy mood.

Above The Hermitage

Left One of the Lake Pavilions

The Temple of Venus:
The unfaithfulness of women

The Temple of Venus is dedicated to the goddess of sex (and of gardening). Again, it was decorated with murals by Sleter (now gone) showing Malbecco peering from behind a tree at his unfaithful wife, as she disports herself with satyrs. In another scene, he tries unsuccessfully to drag her away. In the niches flanking the central portico are busts of the notoriously licentious emperors Nero and Vespasian and the adulteresses Cleopatra and Faustina. The Temple of Venus was designed by William Kent in 1731 and was his first contribution to the garden. It stands at the south-west corner of the garden, where the southern and western stretches of Bridgeman's ha-ha meet, and overlooks the south end of the Eleven-acre Lake.

Above The Temple of Venus

Left Bust of Cleopatra on the Temple of Venus

The Path of Vice

The Queen Caroline Monument: *The divine Caroline*

The plinth and four Ionic columns were probably designed by Vanbrugh to display Rysbrack's statue of Caroline of Anspach, George II's wife. When the South Vista was widened in the 1760s, the monument was moved to its present position at the western end of the Eleven-acre Lake.

The Sleeping Parlour: *Sweet dreams*

This square brick building was hidden away in a mazy woodland wilderness between the Western Garden and the South Vista. It was demolished in 1760. It was inspired by Charles Perrault's famous fairy tale, *Sleeping Beauty*, which had been translated into English in 1710, and was originally topped by urns decorated with grinning faces (symbolising sleep and dreams), which now stand on the Oxford Bridge. In keeping with the mood of this part of the garden, it was inscribed with the motto of the pleasure-loving Epicureans, 'Since all things are uncertain, indulge thyself.'

Left The Queen Caroline Monument

Below The Sleeping Parlour; engraving in the 1750 Seeley guidebook

Opposite The Rotondo

Opposite below The Temple of Bacchus; engraving in the 1750 Seeley guidebook

'Lo! in the Centre of this beauteous Scene,
Glitters beneath her Dome the Cyprian Queen.'

Gilbert West, *Stowe* (1752)

The Rotondo: *Goddess of sex*

A gilded statue of the Medici Venus (West's 'Cyprian Queen') stands beneath the dome of this beautiful circular building, which was designed by Vanbrugh and built in 1720–1. It originally stood at the hub of the Western Garden with avenues radiating out from it towards the Octagon Lake and the Queen Caroline Monument.

From the Rotondo, you can view the sites of three garden buildings that have now disappeared: the Temple of Bacchus, St Augustine's Cave and the Vanbrugh Pyramid.

The Temple of Bacchus: *Drunken lechery*

It was dedicated to Bacchus, god of wine, drunkenness and lechery, and was decorated with murals on these themes. The figure of Bacchus was apparently a portrait of the dissolute Rev. Rand (see p.19). It was demolished in 1926.

The Path of Vice

St Augustine's Cave:
The trials of celibacy

Constructed of tree roots, moss and thatch, this was hidden in woodland behind the Temple of Bacchus. An inscription described St Augustine's failing efforts to keep lust at bay:

> With wondress art a girl of snow
> Did make, the life resembling so
> That one from t'other scarce you'd
> know
> This done the good man side by side
> Lay down t'enjoy his new formed
> bride …

But, frustratingly, the snowwoman literally melted in his arms.

Above right The Vanbrugh
Pyramid; engraving in the
1750 Seeley guidebook

Below right The George II
Monument; engraving in
the 1750 Seeley guidebook

The Vanbrugh Pyramid:
Time to leave

Designed by Vanbrugh, this stepped pyramid
was more like an obelisk. It was erected at the
north-west corner of the garden in 1726 after
the architect's death. Lord Cobham
transformed it into a memorial to Vanbrugh.
It also marked the final stage in the Path of
Vice, as a sober quotation from Horace
inscribed on it made clear:

> You have played, eaten enough and
> drunk enough,
> Now it is time to leave the stage for
> younger men.

Vanbrugh's Pyramid was demolished in 1797.

Dido's Cave:
Hopeless love

The theme here is the doomed love of Dido,
Queen of Carthage, and Aeneas, founder of
Rome, as described in Book VI of Virgil's
Aeneid. According to Virgil, Dido and Aeneas
consummated their love in a cave like this
during a thunderstorm, but Aeneas
subsequently abandoned the Carthaginian
queen to resume his mission. Murals, probably
again by Sleter, described the scene. Dido's
Cave was also known as 'the Randibus' after
the Rev. Conway Rand, who was vicar of
Stowe in the 1740s. 'Rand by name and randy
by nature', he pursued and raped a maid here.
This modest alcove, now largely hidden by
shrubs, was probably built in the 1720s.

The George II Monument

Although Cobham fell out with George II,
siding with Frederick, Prince of Wales, he
still felt that his king deserved a monument
in the garden.

The Path of Virtue

If you turn right from the Lake Pavilions, you will be taking the Path of Virtue, which leads in turn to the related Path of Liberty (see p.26). The Paths of Virtue and Liberty both reflect the family's political views: their love of ancient Greek and Saxon freedoms, and hatred of Roman and modern-day tyranny.

The Elysian Fields:
Earthly paradise

The little valley that lies to the east of the South Vista was originally occupied by the main road from Buckingham. About 1732 the approach to the house was moved to the north so that the valley could be incorporated into the garden. It rapidly became the heart of Stowe, where the grandest *al fresco* entertainments took place.

The valley was christened the Elysian Fields – the paradise of classical mythology. The idea for this part of the garden seems to have been inspired by a 1709 essay by Joseph Addison, in which he described temples dedicated to honour, virtue and vanity in an elysian landscape. The Elysian Fields contain the greatest concentration of garden monuments at Stowe, the strongest political message and the most intense mood. The most prominent features were all designed by William Kent, who may also have conceived the landscape setting. Kent was the pioneer in a new, more

informal style of landscape gardening that took hold in the 1730s and of which the Elysian Fields were a prime example.

The river that runs through the Elysian Fields is divided in two by the Shell Bridge. Below the bridge is the Worthies River, where the landscape is more open, the planting trimmed and the mood sunny. Above the bridge is the Alder River or River Styx (the entrance to the classical underworld), where the foliage is denser and the atmosphere altogether gloomier.

Above The more open, southern end of the Elysian Fields

Opposite above The ruined Temple of Modern Virtue; engraving in the 1750 Bickham guidebook

Opposite below The Doric Arch

'Everything in his deep solitude encourages meditation and inspires melancholy.'

Baron van Spaen van Biljoen, 1791

Temple of Modern Virtue.

The Temple of Modern Virtue:
An age without virtue

Cobham conceived this temple as a ruin – a pointed comment on what he saw as the Walpole regime's lack of virtue. Early engravings show that it also featured a headless statue, which may have been meant as an ironic portrait of Walpole.

The Temple of Ancient Virtue:
Four noble Greeks

The Temple of Ancient Virtue was completed in 1737 to designs by William Kent, who was inspired by the ancient Temple of Vesta at Tivoli. The circular temple form was considered particularly solemn and has inspired many imitations, most famously the Jefferson Monument in Washington DC. Stowe's version contains full-length statues of four ancient Greeks, each of whom was pre-eminent in his own field: the general Epaminondas, the legislator Lycurgus, the poet Homer and the philosopher Socrates. The original statues were sold in 1921, but have been replaced by casts.

Above **Statue of the Greek general Epaminondas**

Below **The Temple of Ancient Virtue**

The Doric or Amelian Arch:
A royal visitor

The Doric Arch was erected in 1768 by Earl Temple to designs by his cousin, Thomas Pitt. This smaller version of the triumphal Corinthian Arch (see p.12) had three functions. It provided a suitably grand entrance to the Elysian Fields. It framed views of the Palladian Bridge and Stowe Castle; and it commemorated a visit by Princess Amelia in 1770: hence its alternative title – the Amelian Arch.

The Path of Virtue

The Grenville Column:
Worthy of Elysium

Cobham's nephew Captain Thomas Grenville was fatally wounded while commanding HMS *Defiance* in a battle with the French off Cape Finisterre in 1747. Cobham put up this column, which is appropriately decorated with ships' prows, in his memory. Captain Grenville was considered to be the member of the family most worthy of a place in Elysium by his brother, Earl Temple, who had the column moved to its present position.

The Grotto:
Al fresco entertainment

This shell- and tufa-encrusted Rococo-style building was designed by William Kent in the 1730s to stand at the head of the gloomy Alder River. It houses a statue of the crouching Venus and served as a small banqueting house, despite the damp.

The perils of outdoor entertainment in July

'The evening was more than cool, and the destined spot [the Grotto] anything but dry. There were not half lamps enough, and no music but an ancient militia-man, who played cruelly on a squeaking tabor and pipe …. I could not help laughing as I surveyed our troop, which, instead of tripping lightly to such an Arcadian entertainment, were hobbling down by the balustrades, wrapped up in cloaks and greatcoats, for fear of catching cold.'

Horace Walpole, 1770

Top The Temple of British Worthies

Above Captain Cook's Monument

Captain Cook's Monument: *Death at sea*

This plinth topped by a globe commemorates Captain Cook's voyages of discovery in the south Pacific in the 1770s and was set up by Earl Temple in 1778. The inscription from the Latin poet Horace tells the story of the Roman sailor Anchites, who, like Cook, was murdered at sea, and because his body was never found, was denied proper burial, being forced to wait 100 years before he could enter Elysium.

The Temple of British Worthies: *Ideas and action*

It was designed by William Kent in 1734–5, based on an unused design for the garden at Chiswick villa in west London. It takes the form of a curved screen with niches for busts of sixteen Britons that Cobham believed deserved commemoration. It is the most overtly political of all the Stowe monuments, with eight men of ideas (on the left) and seven men (and one woman) of action on the right. In the oval niche in the centre is the figure of the messenger god, Mercury, who leads the

virtuous to Elysium. The busts of King Alfred, the Black Prince, John Hampden and William III represent key upholders of ancient British liberties. Elizabeth I, Sir Francis Drake and Sir Walter Ralegh defeated the threat of Catholic tyranny posed by the Spanish Armada in 1588. The only specifically anti-Walpole figure is Sir John Barnard, whose bust was one of the last to be added, by Earl Temple in 1763. The serious message is laced with humour. The back of the central block was meant to hold a statue of 'Signor Fido': 'An Italian of good Extraction; who came into England not to bite us, like most of his Countrymen, but to gain an honest Livelyhood…. Not a Man but a **Grey-hound**.'

William III: 'Who by his Virtue and Constancy, having saved his Country from a foreign Master, by a bold and generous Enterprize, preserv'd the Liberty and Religion of Great Britain.'

The Path of Virtue

'Certain it is … other Nations have never flourish'd
more, in good Laws, Wealth and Conquests, than
under the Administration of Women.'

Viscount Molesworth, 1721

The Queen's Temple:
Virtuous women

Probably designed by James Gibbs about 1742,
it was originally called the Lady's Temple and
was dedicated to female companionship, with
murals depicting such 18th-century feminine
pursuits as shell- and needlework (now gone).
As such, it complemented the Temple of
Friendship, which celebrated male
companionship and can be seen at the
opposite end of Hawkwell Field.

The portico and steps were added in 1772–4
by Earl Temple. In 1790 it was rechristened the
Queen's Temple in honour of Queen Charlotte
after she had nursed her sickly husband,
George III, back to health.

The Cobham Monument:
A truly great man

It was built in 1747–9 by 'Capability' Brown to designs by Gibbs at the end of Lord Cobham's life, and became Cobham's memorial. The octagonal shaft is topped by a small belvedere or viewing platform, which is reached by a spiral staircase. Above that is an over-lifesize statue of Lord Cobham in Roman armour, which was commissioned by his widow. Cobham may have been suspicious of the tyranny of Imperial Rome, but as a soldier he recognised Rome's military prowess. The column recalls those dedicated to two other soldiers: Trajan's Column in Rome and the Victory Column of the Duke of Marlborough at Blenheim. The original statue was shattered by lightning in 1957, and was replaced with a replica in 2001. The tablets round the base are inscribed with quotations from Alexander Pope and a tribute in Latin to Cobham, who was described as 'a truly great man'. Avenues were cut through the surrounding woodland to provide views to the Temple of Concord and Victory and south to the Gothic Temple.

The Chinese House:
A rare survival

The first garden building in England in the Chinese style, it was erected in 1738, originally in the middle of a small pool on stilts near the Elysian Fields. Although very different from the classical buildings that populate the Elysian Fields, it may have been considered an appropriate addition, as an exemplar of Confucian virtue, which was very fashionable in the 1730s. It is little short of miraculous that such a flimsy structure, decorated with Chinese scenes on canvas, should have survived almost three centuries of British weather. Around 1750 it was taken down and moved to the Grenville house at Wotton and then to Ireland, where it remained until 1992, when it was acquired by the National Trust. Because its original setting in the Elysian Fields had disappeared, it was re-erected in the Lamport Gardens. An appeal in memory of Gervase Jackson-Stops, the National Trust's former Architectural Adviser who played a key role in the rescue of Stowe, raised funds for its complete restoration.

Opposite far left
The Queen's Temple

Opposite left
Queen Charlotte; after
Allan Ramsay, 1763 (detail)

Left The Cobham
Monument

Right The Chinese House

The Path of Liberty

Opposite The Grecian
Valley

Below The Temple of
Concord and Victory in
1796–7; watercolour by
Thomas Medland

Below left The pediment of
the Temple of Concord and
Victory is decorated with
sculpture celebrating the
commercial achievements
of the British Empire

The third walk was the last to be created. It occupies the north-east corner of the garden and takes in the Grecian Valley and Hawkwell Field. The theme is the origin of English political liberty in ancient Greece and Anglo-Saxon England.

The Temple of Concord and Victory: *Birthplace of liberty*

Cobham identified Greece as the birthplace of European liberty, and in 1747 built this huge temple (known originally as the Grecian Temple) to honour that nation: it can justly claim to be the first Greek Revival building in England. In 1761–4 it was remodelled and renamed the Temple of Concord and Victory to celebrate British successes in the Seven Years War, in which Temple's brother-in-law, William Pitt the elder, had played a leading part. The pediment, which is topped by a statue of Victory, now contains relief sculpture formerly on the Palladian Bridge on the grand imperial theme of *The Four Quarters of the World bringing their various fortunes to Britannia*.

From here you can enjoy views of the Cobham Monument and the Wolfe Obelisk.

The Grecian Valley: *Brown begins*

This was the last major addition to the garden, and was added at its north-east corner in the 1740s. It was also a key project in the early career of 'Capability' Brown, who in 1741 was appointed head gardener and clerk of works, responsible not only for the planting, but also for the upkeep of the garden buildings. Brown embarked on a massive earth-moving campaign to create the Grecian Valley, which slopes away gently from the front of the temple and is enclosed by belts of trees.

Stowe can justly claim to be the birthplace of the English landscape style, as Brown went on to apply the principles he had learnt here to numerous parks and gardens across Britain.

Inset 'Capability' Brown, who was head gardener at Stowe from 1741 to 1751 and created the Grecian Valley; by Nathaniel Dance, c.1769

The Wolfe Obelisk:
Hero of the Seven Years War

General Wolfe's victory at Quebec in 1759 had secured Canada for the British Empire, and his death at the moment of triumph had transformed him into a national hero. Wolfe had been a friend of Earl Temple and had dined with him on the evening before he set off for Canada. The obelisk had originally stood in the middle of the Octagon Lake and was moved to its present position in the deer-park north of the garden in 1754.

The Bourbon Tower:
Exiles and exercises

Known originally as the Gothic Tower, it was built of the same local orange Northamptonshire ironstone to serve as a gamekeeper's lodge. In 1804 it was renamed the Bourbon Tower after the exiled French royal family, who were living nearby and visited Stowe. The Buckinghamshire Yeomanry, commanded by the Duke of Buckingham, used it as a mock fort during their military exercises.

The Path of Liberty

'Gods of a nation, valiant, wise and free,
Who conquer'd to establish Liberty!
To whose auspicious Care Britannia owes
Those Laws on which she stands, by which she rose.'

Gilbert West, *Stowe* (1752)

The Saxon Deities:
Gods of our ancestors

Arranged in a circle are replicas of six of the seven Portland stone statues of the Saxon gods that gave their names to the days of the week: Sunna, Mona, Tw, Woden, Thuner, Friga and Seatem. These Saxon gods were associated with the ancient liberties of Britain and were part of the Germanic political heritage that the British shared with the Hanoverian dynasty, which had ruled the country since 1714. The original statues were carved by J.M. Rysbrack.

Hawkwell Field:
East of Eden

Hawkwell Field, which lies to the east of the Elysian Fields, was brought within the garden in the late 1730s. The buildings erected here, which were all designed by Gibbs, are larger and more spaciously arranged than those in the Elysian Fields, but with the same attention to their relationships. They also proclaim Cobham's Whig Protestant views. The setting is more informal and pastoral, with sheep being allowed to roam freely.

'High on a summit all below commands,
Fair *Liberty* thy destin'd *temple* stands.'

Samuel Boyse, *The Triumphs of Nature* (1742)
on the Gothic Temple

Opposite The Saxon god Woden

Left The Gothic Temple

Below The domed ceiling of the Gothic Temple

The Gothic Temple:
Liberty revived

It is unusual for Stowe in being built in the Gothic style, to a triangular plan, and from Northamptonshire ironstone. The inscription in French translates as: 'I thank God that I am not a Roman.' For Cobham wanted to contrast Roman tyranny with British liberty as it was championed by the Saxons such as King Alfred (who appears on the Temple of British Worthies; see p.23) and the Earls of Mercia. The building is dedicated to 'the liberties of our Ancestors'. The domed ceiling is painted with heraldic shields that trace the Temple family's lineage back to their Saxon forebears. Like most of the temples in Hawkwell Field, it was designed by James Gibbs (in 1741, but was not complete by 1748).

The Gothic Temple is now leased by the Landmark Trust, which rents it out as a holiday cottage.

'Pure and beautiful and venerable.'
Horace Walpole on the Gothic Temple

The Path of Liberty

'… if a Sudden Shower interrupts your Walk you here find a Shelter from the Water above you. A good Bridge that not only carrys one safe over, but also dry, under the Water.'

A visitor to Stowe in 1738

The Palladian Bridge:
Safe shelter

The covered bridge at the east end of the Octagon Lake was designed to enable the family and its guests to enjoy a circular carriage drive around the edge of Hawkwell Field. Probably designed by Gibbs and completed in 1736, it is the second of three very similar bridges built in English country-house gardens in the early 18th century. The design has nothing to do with the 16th-century north Italian architect Andrea Palladio, but was probably the work of Roger Morris, who built the prototype at Wilton House in Wiltshire. Another early example is also in the care of the National Trust, at Prior Park in Bath.

Below The Palladian Bridge

Left The Temple of Friendship

Below Stowe Castle: engraving from the 1750 Bickham guide

The Temple of Friendship:
Political parties

Dedicated to male friendship, it stands on the bastion at the east end of Bridgeman's ha-ha, balancing the Temple of Venus at the opposite end, which is dedicated to less respectable pleasures. It also complements the Queen's Temple at the other end of Hawkwell Field, which was the domain of Lady Cobham and her female friends.

The Temple of Friendship was built by Gibbs in the early 1740s to accommodate supper parties held by Lord Cobham and his male friends and relations. These parties had a strong political flavour, particularly after 1733, when Cobham and his cousins ('the Boy Patriots') broke with the Prime Minister, Sir Robert Walpole. Their hero was Frederick, Prince of Wales, the son of George II and father of George III, but never king himself, who stayed at Stowe in 1727. A marble bust of the Prince was once displayed inside the temple alongside busts of Lord Cobham, Earl Temple and their political circle. The ceiling was decorated with murals symbolising male friendship, justice and liberty. The building was damaged by fire in the 1840s and has remained a roofless ruin ever since.

Stowe Castle

From Hawkwell Field you get good views of the castellated silhouette of Stowe Castle (actually a humble farmstead) on the horizon in the deer-park to the east. This pseudo-medieval eye-catcher recalls the era of Magna Carta and the Barons' Wars, which helped to establish Britain's traditional liberties.

Castle

Looking to the Future

Working with the Stowe House Preservation Trust (owners and custodians of Stowe House), the National Trust has achieved a huge amount since it took over responsibility for the gardens in 1990. Lakes have been dredged, historic vistas re-opened, thousands of trees and shrubs planted, and Stowe's famous garden buildings and sculptures restored or re-created. Significant outlying elements of the designed landscape have been acquired, and the vast archive of Stowe papers has been researched. But since 1990, visitors have had to enter the gardens at their north-east corner through temporary buildings.

The New Inn

Now, thanks to the acquisition of the New Inn and a generous grant of £1.5 million from the Heritage Lottery Fund, you can once again follow the magnificent traditional approach to the gardens and enjoy Stowe as it was meant to be seen. The project will offer a greatly enriched experience for visitors. A vibrant new

Left Carving a new capital for the Temple of Concord and Victory

Below left The New Inn after restoration

Visitor Centre has been created in what until recently had been a derelict farmhouse and posting inn, which had been used by the earliest visitors to Stowe around 300 years ago. By transforming the visitor experience, you will enjoy a greater understanding of what it would have been like to visit Stowe in its 18th-century heyday.

A work in progress

The restoration of the New Inn is only the most recent in an ambitious programme of work. Much more remains to be done at Stowe, repairing its unrivalled group of garden buildings, and reviving its historic landscape. With your help, the National Trust will make it happen.